A Prophet in the Moment

Understanding Where You Are At In The Prophetic Process

Ken Cox

Copyright © 2019 by Ken Cox

All rights reserved. No part of this publication may be reproduced by any means, graphics, electronic, or mechanical, including photocopying, recording, taping, or by any information storage retrieval system without the written permission of the publisher except in the case of brief quotations embodied in critical articles and reviews.

Ken Cox/Rejoice Essential Publishing

PO BOX 512

Effingham, SC 29541

www.republishing.org

Author's website: https://www.whereeaglesfly.us

Unless otherwise indicated, scripture is taken from the King James Version.

Scripture quotation marked (NIV) taken from the Holy Bible, New International Version®, NIV®. Copyright © 1973, 1978, 1984, 2011 by Biblica, Inc.™ Used by permission of Zondervan. All rights reserved worldwide. www.zondervan.com

Scripture quotation marked (ESV) taken from The Holy Bible, English Standard Version® (ESV®) Copyright © 2001 by Crossway, a publishing ministry of Good News Publishers. All rights reserved.

A Prophet In The Moment/ Ken Cox

ISBN-10: 1-946756-58-X

ISBN-13: 978-1-946756-58-9

Library of Congress Control Number: 2019907980

Table of Contents

INTRODUCTION..1

CHAPTER 1:   Prophetic Integrity..........5

CHAPTER 2:   When a Prophet Leaves Zigzag.................16

CHAPTER 3:   The Prophets Process of Transfer.........28

CHAPTER 4:   The Championship Prophet..........................38

CHAPTER 5:   The Prophet, Called or Chosen.............49

CHAPTER 6:   What's Your Relationship with Prophetic Money...........59

CHAPTER 7:   The investment of a Prophetic Friend............................82

CHAPTER 8: Prophets and
The
Good-Bye Gift..................95

FINAL THOUGHT..108

ABOUT THE AUTHOR.................................110

Introduction

Have you ever taken the time to look around today at the Body of Christ? We are so divided in the prophetic ministry that it appears that our best efforts only seemingly unite pockets of us here and there. We, the prophets, don't trust each other, never build the relationships needed to prosper in the prophetic gift and never seem to understand the benefit of prophetic transfer.

There is much to discuss on this point. Hurt, anger, and self-esteem are the front runners of the walls between us. We also have a more unspoken division that we can't see, but we know it is there. Welcome to the moments of life we are called to as prophets of God. Please realize now this is bigger than your local circles of influence but important to you and them nevertheless.

Today it seems many prophets seek to form relationships based on the norms of today's society. We are living in the moment, an unfulfilled moment, that has us yearning for the supernatural and never see it consistently, and when we do, it's only a moment, now and then.

Yes, my prophetic friend..., can I call you friend? Notice that we are living in the moment, one right after the other. We must take our responsibility to understand the moments. Do our actions and works as prophets bring Glory or disgrace to the Kingdom of God? This is a fair question each of us should ask ourselves.

While we deal with the world of today, try to find ourselves, and look to who we feel is the latest media prophetic superstar. There is a need to realize that all platforms of our society will not change unless we, the prophets bring God's Glory to those places for God. What I'm describing is a lost gift among us at this moment. Yet it is ageless and essential to our continued development as prophets. Welcome to the moment in time, many of us need to realize, embrace and cherish, even with all our shortcomings. This is an excellent opportunity to grow a prophet.

My task in the following chapters is to outline moments we all will deal with. These topics are essential to us surviving and thriving as prophets of God. Our sensitivity to the issues of life and the areas we so often overlook makes us so non effective. My goal with this book is to challenge you to understand, claim, and excel at the moment you find yourself in. This is for you, the prophet, and the person you are. My prayer is that they become one and the same.

Everything we deal with is a process. Claim this as a real prophet. Just when you felt you had learned everything you needed to know about being a prophet- there is even more to learn. We all are a part of some prophetic subculture.

Our culture binds us and in some cases our counterculture.

These have a direct bearing on our individual and group norms and especially our prophetic standards. As we look at ourselves, at the moment we find ourselves in. We all strive to find a reference point. Sometimes it's in a positive sense of identity. Sometimes it is not. Ask yourself, Can I identify it? Can I develop from it?

This book is going to offer subjects that you will find critical in your prophetic development. Study yourself as you read this book and be honest with yourself. The subject matter of this book is real and authentic. I speak to you in this work, as a prophet and a future prophetic friend.

I submit to you, "A Prophet in the Moment." You and I had better be ready and available to deal with it. The moment is here for us, and the beautiful saga here is that we, the prophets of God, have a chance to make a difference. Prophet, you and I are in the moment, as we seek our greatest lives in God. You and I are "A Prophet in the Moment."

CHAPTER 1

Prophetic Integrity

Have you ever smiled at someone and felt a particular type of way about them? Today in the body of Christ, we the prophets, whether we want to realize it, can't keep ignoring the fact that, there is a colossal integrity problem in the Body of Christ and within our prophetic ranks. As a leader, I've seen this and dealt with it. I watched my peers suffer, fail, and praised God for those who were victimized and yet prevailed. Every relevant prophet in some way will have this as a deposited experience. You will not be able to run from this. People and prophets will lie to you and on you.

The prophetic ranks are suffering from integrity which is disturbing, especially regarding us who speak for God. Where are the Jeremiah prophets of today, who will call out the prophetic peers as Jeremiah did and tell them how to live, lives of integrity? Are we too intimidated by our out of order peers?

Have you ever noticed as we work so hard to be friends with each other, we are not friendly enough to tell our brother, or sister, or prophetic friend something that may help them out? We need to connect to find a real outreach, of prophets, who will be practical enough to walk in the Jeremiah integrity.

Today, many still have a problem realizing God has restored apostles and prophets to the end time church, that we are a part of. Why do you think our ability to police ourselves and make our whole better is lost? It's because we are being fought by the very ones who we should be working with and standing side by side with?

Is it our job is to proclaim the present the biblical truth boldly to guide the church into the establishment of God's rule and kingdom upon the world? This question is designed to make us, think and look at ourselves first.

Why is there a lack of investment in knowing Gods ways? We must be eager to display and have the word of God demonstrated in our lives, moment by moment. You and I, we are still the prophets of God regardless of what some may say. That will not change.

So, my prophetic friend, what I'm talking about will propel us; beyond, what we are comfortable with. This is how we will and must grow. This is also a vital issue to the prophetic perspective of working with prophets and prophetic people. Prophets must allow God to trust them with the Rhema (Spirit). This is because the prophet must be confident in the logos (written word) of God. Being confident will allow us to seek growth in the Word of God.

This is not about the picking up and putting down of the prophetic mantle when it fits, when the camera is on, or when it is offering time, and the little old lady has a one or two comma check for us. We are prophets in every moment. We must understand the moment. That's the issue, and our integrity and character are on display, big time.

None of us is everyone's prophet, nor are we everyone's mentor. The point is, many of us today are not true to ourselves and are incapable of being true to anyone. The sad fact is that many times it is the one that God has put you in covenant or assignment with, which we are untrue to. This is all while we try to be everyone's prophet and mentor. Please stop that today.

Let's look at integrity as a firm adherence to a code of moral values, which donates soundness and incorruptibility. For a prophet, prophetic integrity is the mother of prophetic virtue as we deal justly with ourselves, not others, ourselves.

We are in a moment, and we must get a handle on ourselves before we can even attempt to understand and mentor our prophetic peers.

Prophets, there are three critical elements of integrity. First, there is dealing justly with oneself, which is the inner prophet. Secondly, there is dealing justly with others like our peers. Thirdly and finally, we recognizing integrity is, therefore, the quality or condition of being whole, complete, unbroken, and undivided. We should desire to be one with God. Does this fit in your prophetic lifestyle?

Prophets, who are willing to deal justly with themselves, are the prophets who lay a foundation for dealing rightly with others. Performance of duty, regardless of the sacrifice involved, is a part of dealing justly with oneself and others. Prophetic integrity means that we do what is right and good, regardless of the immediate consequences. Prophets, this means being righteous from the very depth of your soul, not only in your actions but, more importantly, in your thoughts and your heart. Now you know this is not easy to do especially when you're mad and upset, let's get real now!

Honesty is the prophetic quality or condition that ensures the prophet is truthful, sincere, candid, and worthy of growing in his or her gift. A prophet with integrity means the prophet is honorable, speaking the truth, whether the world receives it or not, and that includes themselves.

Prophetic integrity becomes the value we set on ourselves through the word of God as we adhere to it. This is how we fulfill our duty as prophets of God. An honorable prophet will personally commit to living up to certain self-imposed expectations, as they are distinguished to the core of their being. This type of prophet lives according to a single, consistent set of ethics, in every area of their life.

The prophet Jeremiah showed us when we follow different ethical precepts, in various spheres of life, we lack integrity. He saw a lack of integrity in the people of Judah. They, like many of us today, seemed to believe that they could violate God's ethical norms in work and daily life. We show up to service, as the same way they came to the temple, acting holy and saved. They, like us today, seemed to have no fear of the consequences of their actions. When we make vows, we ignore them, and get an attitude or make accusations when questioned. We are the today people of Judah and not the prophets of God.

Numbers 30:2 (ESV) says, "Moses said, "If a man vows a vow unto the Lord or swear an oath to bind his soul with a bond; he shall not break his word, he shall do according to all that proceeds out of his mouth."

Prophet you must process this kind of integrity; it is the light of a disciplined conscience. It is the strength of duty within us.

Today, let us look at ourselves. We are prophets and being true to oneself at times requires extraordinary strength and courage. Our God, who makes and keeps His covenants, he can be trusted (1 Chronicles 16:15; Psalm 105:8).

He, our God, is trustworthy. We can and must strive to be like our God. Our character is not just words; our character walks hand in hand with our prophetic integrity. This is bigger than doing the right thing. It is a matter of having the right heart and allowing the person you are on the inside to match the person you project on the outside. This is how God is. This is how the prophet should be. This is how the Prophet must be.

Think about this, "Till I die I will not remove mine integrity from me (Job 27:5)." The great Job had lost almost everything he valued: family, friends, health, and wealth. Job refused to give up his integrity. Prophets, do we trade away our integrity? This is a question for us to ponder? How do we handle ourselves? Our integrity is beyond price; it is invaluable.

Joseph was a Seer and a model of prophetic integrity. He did the right thing. Looking at his life, we see a prophet who was trustworthy, incorruptible, and self-disciplined, and has never violated a trust. Because of his integrity and righteousness, Joseph was favored and blessed of the Lord in every circumstance. His life is evidence that "all things work together for good to [those who] love God (Rom. 8:28)."

In Daniel 2:28, we see Daniel as he reflects his ability to walk in integrity, which paved the way for him to receive the respect and affection of the powerful Kings he served under. He never compromised his faith. Daniel's honesty and loyalty were to God. This was prophetic integrity at its best.

We must learn total obedience to God. Prophetic ministry requires a high standard of holiness. Have you figured that out yet? 1 Kings 13:22-25 enlightens us to the story of the young prophet, who started well, but ended in disaster because he failed to obey the word that God had spoken to him.

All prophets should read this chapter frequently, but do we? 1 Kings 13:21 says, "You have defied the word of the Lord and have not kept the command the Lord your God gave you. You came back and ate bread and drank water in the place where he told you not to eat or drink. Therefore, your body will not be buried in the tomb of your fathers." This sounds like today's prophetic movement in a lot of aspects.

Are we like Elisha as he trained to become a prophet? He learned obedience. In 1 Kings 19:21, Elisha is called into the prophetic. He leaves Elijah and goes back to his people. He took his yoke of oxen and slaughtered them. This happens all while Elijah was telling him to go back. Welcome to understanding the moment. He burned the plowing equipment to cook the meat and, gave it to the people, and they ate. Then he set out to follow Elijah and became his attendant. That's Integrity. He handled his business.

Mature prophets are so in love with God and submitted to Him; their integrity is almost beyond questioning. I had to learn that the Word of the Lord shall come to you; not for my sake alone, but for those to whom I would be sent to.

Prophet, God demands of you, total, absolute consecration to His purpose and willingness to go on an errand on which He may send. Prophetic integrity begins the moment you, die to the world prophet! Philippians 1:20 says, "A dead man is a dangerous man." He cannot be intimidated or threatened. The reality of us being dead to the world is real to God, as He can share and allow us to see the moments, we find ourselves in.

As Prophets, you may have a brand. It is not your attire, habits, or lifestyle as a prophet. It is your consistent ministry backed up with holiness of God's character. Am I talking to you now? Prophet are we demonstrating with our lives that we are at peace with God? You now become a prophetic mouthpiece of maturity as you speak out of your relationship with God and not out of reaction to a situation. That's mature prophetic integrity. Welcome to growth, as we siege the moment, God has us in.

CHAPTER 2

When A Prophet Leaves Ziklag

There is a time in every life when we get tired. We start to feel like we can't go on. We get frustrated. We feel humiliated. We feel like we will never get there. This chapter is for prophetic leaders and prophets who are looking for and who seek to discover their prophetic destiny.

Some prophets feel like they are stuck and not appreciated. Some prophets are worried, shattered, and broken. Let's look at David. He provides us with an example of life activity that God will only invest in a leader, who He has plans for. David, while fleeing from King Saul, David joined the Philistines, ancient Israel's bitter enemies. With 600 men and their families, David, with his family, presented himself to Achish, King of the Philistine city of Gath, to ask for asylum.

Achish gave David the town of Ziklag, and he lived there a year and four months. Ziklag was the base of his operations and where he, had his family, and the 600 other men lived while he fought with the Philistines. He felt like he accomplished something but let's look deeper into the character of Ziklag.

Welcome to Ziklag. This is the place where, like David, you are going from one thing to another. The storms of life seem to embrace, encamp, and force you into desperate action. David had a backlog of issues, pain and trouble in a short time and was faced with a deal, which he was unsure of.

In 1 Samuel 27, David, his men, and their families are tired. We now have Achish said to David, "You know, of course, that you and your men are to go out with me in the army.'" David said to Achish, "Very well, then you shall know what your servant can do." 'Achish said to David, "Very well, I will make you my bodyguard for life." David is in a place of unsureness in his spirit. He has had been running for his life and now it seemed like he had to run to the very place he was working to destroy before the conflict came to his life.

Welcome prophet to your Ziklag. This is a place of rest, but a place of worry. This is a place of stress but, you are expected to find calmness. You're in Ziklag, and you're hanging on by a thread. If the wind blows a certain way, it will only destroy you. Ziklag is the place of your transition from a follower to a leader. In your Ziklag, you are close to your enemy, yet you're not hurt. , You're doing on the job training for your mantle.

After almost two years, David was released from the obligation by Achish. He has served under pressure well, but he was not trusted to move forth. After his release, we see David and his men returned to Ziklag.

And it came to pass when David and his men were come to Ziklag on the third day, that the Amalekites had invaded the south, and Ziklag, and smitten Ziklag, and burned it with fire; And had taken the women captives that were therein: they slew not any, either great or small, but carried them away, and went on their way. So David and his men came to the city, and, behold, it was burned with fire, and their wives, and their sons, and their daughters were taken captives. Then David and the people that were with him lifted their voice and wept until they had no more power to weep. And David's two wives were taken captives, Ahinoam the Jezreelites, and Abigail, the wife of Nabal the Carmelite. And David was greatly distressed; for the people spoke of stoning him because the soul of all the people was grieved, every man for his sons and his daughters: but David encouraged himself in the Lord his God. – 1 Samuel 30:1-6

Again, David was sick, tired, frustrated, and worried. Those who were with him were now against him. This is geared to reach out to prophetic leaders, and emerging prophets who God is raising. David was in a position like many prophetic leaders. You must learn how to encourage yourself. What do I mean? You must strengthen yourself in The Lord. Prophet, you're in your lives, strangest battles and yet you will only listen to the calm, quiet voice of God, despite the situation. Am I talking to you?

David's situation shows us that there will be situations where you have given and done your best but, the odds of success and the outlook of the battle will look like they are against you. The issue here is that you may be wounded, but you always must go forth. There is nothing that will come against you that can proper!

Many of today's prophets must realize that we are wounded. Prophet, your wound will not be healed by accepting the defeat, the loss, and forgetting who you are in God. The realm of impossibility is the place we come out of our Ziklag. There is a lesson here for the prophet to learn from David as we raise the level of our relationship with God.

David did not look at his activities, nor did he have to remind God of his encounters with Goliath! David knew who he was, and the type of relationship he had with God. Prophet, have we examined ourselves lately? You and I are locked in our personal Ziklag for a reason.

Like David, you're tired, sleepy, and exhausted but you still must go forth. People are talking about you, saying this and that. Guess what? You still must go forth. Six hundred men who were with him when he was in the Philistine army, who wanted to kill him, now must follow him again. But some of them are far too tired. How about that?

Sometimes there will be people who are not really for you. They want you to get them to a certain point. They were going to leave and betray you anyway. They had plans that were opposite of yours anyway.

One thing you must understand is that along the way, you will face battle after, battle. After a struggle, you will face disappointment and fear. This is for your chosen season. As you develop in your Ziklag just like David, you are facing one thing after another. The actual colors of people in your life show up and show out while God has you at your Ziklag. As a prophet, along the way to your Ziklag, you will have many people who will attempt to attach to your life, but they can't go with you. David saw that half of his army was too tired to travel any more with him, but he still had to wage war with the Amalekites.

David had that kind of relationship with God that allowed him to gear up for the battle, despite his issues and his peers' issues. This is what the prophet of today need. We need that relationship that when everybody is walking away from our life, we can stand up and say, "I must move forth."

Everybody who can't go with you along the way is not a candidate for rebuke, nor are they a candidate for your company either. Prophetic leaders, sometimes you have to go forth, and wish people well. David loved his men, but he had to keep moving. When people in your life, walk as far with you as they can walk, this is not your cue to sit and baby them. You must keep going.

Stop feeling guilty, because you did not quit. Stop feeling guilty because you're perusing your prophetic destiny. Stop allowing people to say they mean well and as long as you fit their model of success, you're anointed. When you don't fit their model of excellence, you're not of God. Prophet, continue to push forward in what God has called you to do.

David is ready to fight anyway. He has fewer men, and the burden is for him to do more. Do you understand, prophet that in this season, God requires you to do more with less? David fights the Amalekites and destroys them. The lesson here is to use what you got have left. David is now coming back from the battle and back to Ziklag.

The Ziklag process also shows us who David is and the character of a God-sent leader. When David returned back to Ziklag, he allowed those who did not participate in the battle with the Amalekites to recover all also. He did not have to, but he did what would reunite his men. There is no doubt all were not happy, but who could argue with the results?

Sometimes God will bring people back into your life, people who have done you wrong, who have misjudged you, and tried to destroy you. He wants you to bless them. Welcome to the Ziklag process.

On the third day after David and his men returned to Ziklag and after their victory over the Amalekites, a messenger arrived with the news of Saul's and Jonathan's deaths. David asks about the circumstances.

David listened to how his former mentor, wounded Saul, then asked the messenger to finish him off. 2 Samuel 1:10 (ESV), "So I stood over him and killed him because I knew that after he had fallen, he could not survive. And I took the crown that was on his head and the band on his arm and have brought them here to my lord."

The messenger probably expected a reward for his mercy killing, but he clearly did not understand what Ziklag had done for David, as he brings David the crown. David mourned. 2 Samuel 1:11-12 (NIV), "Then David and all the men with him took hold of their clothes and tore them. They mourned and wept and fasted till evening for Saul and his son Jonathan, and the army of the LORD and the house of Israel, because they had fallen by the sword."

Prophet, if you don't feel a sense of loss, especially when someone you had a conflict with dies or is killed, something in you needs to be examined. The reality is, in the prophetic, today, we all may not get along, but we need to be able to honor and respect each other., We all may not fellowship, but we need to recognize and honor, the calling upon a man or a woman's life.

David was in the situation he was in now because of Saul, and yet he honored the anointed of God. 2 Samuel 1:14-16 (NIV) says, "David asks the Amalekite, 'Why were you not afraid to lift your hand to destroy the LORD's anointed.' Then David called one of his men and said, 'Go, strike him down!' So he struck him down, and he died. For David had said to him, 'Your blood be on your own head. Your own mouth testified against you when you said, "I killed the LORD's anointed."

Even when Saul had acted un-righteously, David would not slay him, though twice he could have. This opportunist who took killing Saul upon himself was an abomination to David! Being an Amalekite probably doesn't didn't help since David had just finished slaying hundreds of Amalekites whom he considered to be the "enemies of God's people.

Ziklag is the place, where God delays and detains you. It's, the place where you're molded into a leader. Also, it is the place where you're being fine-tuned is on a schedule. God is bringing you out like he brought David out. You're going to have more faith, more anointing, and more commitment. David found out the promise of God. God met him in the place of his most significant pain. Somebody say "The Ziklag process."

The crown, which is, symbolic of the leadership of Israel, has now met David in Ziklag. Prophet, if you can trust God in the place of your greatest failure, you will see your mantle in its greatest manifestation in your place of Ziklag.

CHAPTER 3

The Prophets Process of Transfer

You did not become a prophet, by yourself. You became a prophet because you received something from someone a prophetic word that inspired you, an inspiration, or a thought. This is a type of transfer that will change your life.

Here we see the textbook definition of transfer which is, to convey or remove from one place, person, etc., to another. Also, it is to cause to pass from one person to another, as thought, qualities, or power; transmit. Elisha can testify as well as others to this.

Sometimes prophets will hear things and not be mature enough to understand what they are receiving. When revelation is hindered by immaturity, we will not be able to receive. The prophet's inability to recognize his or her lack of experience will be the prophet's biggest hindrance in growth. Therefore, the transfer is necessary.

Everything is the result of all that has gone before or happened to us is the totality of who we are today. Someone somewhere has deposited in us, as a prophet, and this is why we are, who we are. In other words, they transferred something to us. Ever notice that some prophets are always on the receiving end and never giving and then some are always giving. As prophets mature, we become givers. You as a prophet will reach the place of maturity and understand why you learned that you're gifted to be the blessing to pass on. Immature prophets will have problems with this.

We are as prophets in one of those developmental stages. We must understand that God has made the world in such a manner, that what we get as far as impartation, wisdom, knowledge, or a special anointing or gift are all given through transfer. The enemy wants the prophet to be a maverick, thinking her or she is an island all to themselves, no relationships or no transfer.

Do you ever wonder why, we hear people saying all the time "God has given me this revelation, or that revelation?" It's because as long as we can convince ourselves, we only need us, we will forfeit the benefits of relationships. When we forfeit our relationships, we will lose our, ability to receive the transfer God has for us.

God's plan was and is the same. But when the prophet is isolated, there is no transfer unless God is the one who has separated that prophet and not the work of the enemy. Attitudes, perceptions, envy, strife, everyday old customs, and traditions work for the enemy to isolate the prophet, then they miss the benefit of transfer.

God works through his prophets to help grow other prophets. We saw this in the Biblical Prophetic schools of Elijah, Elisha, Samuel, and others. God wants his prophets to have the gifts, The workings and operations of the gifts are to be distributed by other prophets. This is why God will send 'Prophetic Doorkeepers of Destiny' into the lives of other prophets. These type prophets are the keepers of God's destiny, and they open the doors to prophets who will qualify for transfer.

Whether you like this type of prophet or not, that is not up for question or is it optional. Sometimes God will allow your destiny to be connected to a prophet, you may not like or may not understand, but somehow you must deal with him or her because they have the key to unlocking your destiny. It is not the situation that will get you. It is how you deal with the situation, which is more important because it identifies who you are.

Most of us as prophets fail to build the relationships we need to develop because we feel we don't need anyone except God. That is true, but your mantle transfer, gifting development, and your maturing for the assignment, will come from a prophet, which God has assigned. That is the only place you may get that transfer.

This is a God assignment, not a good old boy or man made assignment. God is not going to allow you or any prophet to access all of Him, unless you go through some other prophet, which He has approved.

Give, and it shall be given unto you; good measure, pressed down, and shaken together, and running over, shall men give into your bosom. For with the same measure that ye mete withal, it shall be measured to you again. —Luke 6:38

Give, and it shall be given to you again; good measure, pressed down, and shaken together. Imagine how many prophets God will send into your life to provide you with that something you need.

God says that when you give, you open the doors of the prophetic transfer. What you give is what you can expect back. We forge relationships that transfer through our giving. The mantles open up and the gift it transferred for the benefit of God's people.

This is why the spirit of the agreement is critical. You will come to understand Matthew 18:19, "Again I say unto you, that if two of you shall agree on earth as touching anything that they shall ask, it shall be done for them of my Father which is in heaven."

When you can come into agreement, the transfer is exchanged. The understanding here is that money is a tool or, not an end to all means as some in the body of Christ wants to make it. Prophets who will not sow or who will not come into an agreement will always have a problem with money. They will blame the transfer of the mantles, gifts, and talents on money solely. Again, the enemy does not want you to get the transfer.

This is why you're isolated, or at odds with everyone. Because you can't receive the transfer, you will always be at a level beneath where God has mandated you should be. In 1 Kings 19, the great Elisha was able to recognize who he was to agree with. This is so critical because that prophet has your transfer for your destiny. Sometimes you have to step away from what your familiar with to understand your destiny and the transfer that is needed.

Have you ever wondered why people such as prophets, friends, enemies, coworkers, or church members keep coming into your life to pull you back into your past? Whoever will pull you back, prophet, is working for the enemy at full throttle. Notice that Elijah had no bearing on the past of Elisha. The only people who have his history in mind were his family and his servants.

Elijah had come to throw the mantle on Elisha to thrust him into his destiny. You are not assigned for transfer, if all you bring are past failures, hurts, and disappointments. Are you the female prophet, who always seems to choose the wrong type of man? Or maybe you're the male prophet who always gets distracted by a particular kind of female. Be careful of shared history because; they do not have your transfer. You may be comfortable, but you will not grow. Know who is around you.

Notice that Elijah made Elisha uncomfortable and he still pushed forward. Growth is uncomfortable. Comfort will destroy your call; it will sour and dull your anointing. Growth is not for you to become familiar, it is for you to get the transfer. This is a mistake Elijah did not allow Elisha to make. There is a need to stretch. There is a need to reach. There is a need to be uncomfortable. Notice that Elijah immediately challenged Elisha because, he had his destiny.

There is a distance between the two prophets that is seen today and often ignored. Today the now generation prophet seems to feel he or she can arrive at their destiny in a shorter time than others. The reality is some will because of obedience. You will soon see those who choose to practice disobedience, by doing things the way that does not challenge or stretch them. They will become jealous and unteachable. They will miss the transfer that they so desperately need.

You will continue to see this prophet in a grand chase of perception and words repeatedly. You will see them post the joy and greatness of the Lord on social media, but growth becomes a lost tale of how they were done wrong and talked to. They will criticize the challenge but never address the lack of their response to the challenge. The answer to the challenge is critical not the challenge. Elisha teaches us that.

Elisha saw that he was connected to a destiny that had his total history, when Elijah passed by him, he saw his destiny. He knew he needed the transfer that Elijah had for him. In his mind, he claimed the transfer. He was going to do nothing else until he got it. What has happened to the prophets of today? Who will not receive the transfer? We seem to think the anointing is taught. No, the anointing is caught.

Who is ready to leave your history? Forget those things that are behind and reach things you have never had before. Who wants a transfer? Who is ready for prophetic transfer? Who is so busy trying to be someone? Who has connected with your history?

Maybe you want to be like Elisha. When he saw his destiny, he moved forth. He gave up being someone in charge, to be a servant or, basically a butler, for Elijah. The issue is that Elijah is a stranger to him, but the relationship with God has connected him to something bigger than him. The situation you're in now is connected to your history, but when God shows you your destiny, will you do as Elisha and break loose and not look back? Your future is too important to ignore. The transfer you need is before you.

Elijah was everything that Elisha was to become. He sowed into the Elijah. He served Elijah and he received the transfer. The connection of transfer is critical to the prophet. God is about getting his gifts and talents to us through transfer, from other prophets. Just as God connected with Adam through transfer, God breathed into him, and he became a living being. Today, God is sending a prophet to you to connect you to your destiny.

CHAPTER 4

The Championship Prophet

What is a champion? The dictionary defines a champion many ways, but one such was as a person who fights or argues for a cause or on behalf of someone else. That sounds like us as prophets. Other terms used are synonyms like advocate, proponent, promoter, proposer, supporter, standard-bearer, torch-bearer, defender, protector, upholder, backer, exponent, patron, sponsor, prime, mover, pleader for, campaigner for, lobbyist for, fighter for, battler for, crusader for, apostle, prophet, evangelist, missionary, and booster. All of these terms can be used to describe a champion. Imagine that.

Is there such thing as a Championship Prophet? Would a prophet treat the call of the prophetic as some type of contest? Does winning in life means different things to different people. Winning in the prophetic is winning in life, for a prophet. We live daily in the prophetic to win in life every day. This is how we learn to deal with our issues as prophets. We live, to win as we learn how to establish a championship mind-set or mentality. What does that mean for a prophet?

What is it, that separates God's prophets from within the ranks of those He will use and those whom he He may choose to use in another way or not use at all? Then there are those whom will not allow themselves to be used of God. There are several mental qualities that you can find in very successful prophets, which distinguish them from their peers.

For a prophet, the key to becoming a champion is how they respond to adversity. When the proverbial crap hits the fan or when things start going very wrong, real championship anointed prophets take all of this in stride, and they keep moving forth.

Some prophets exhibit the uncanny ability not to let people, spirits, or the schemes of the enemy knock them off their center of focus. There is no doubt this takes a level of earned maturity, but even with that, it is a wonder how quickly, a prophet may bounce back, especially after a setback.

Moses, Abraham, and Joseph had this calm. Other prophet of championship caliber response to adversity is practiced, in the presence of God. This comes with the understanding that the problem isn't the problem. The question is how you, the prophet, react to the issue at hand.

A Prophet In The Moment

Championship level prophets know that there are a variety of things that happen that can and will happen that are directly out of their control. They also know that these uncontrollable events are upsetting and distracting. The championship prophet has figured out that it's not the issue itself that hurts. It is the prophet's response to that issue that carries the weight of the solution. Prophet, you can't control uncontrollable, but you can learn to control your reaction to uncontrollable.

Society trains its champions to systematically imagine things going wrong both before and during his performances, and then "practice" successfully coping with each thing that went wrong. In this way, we see that some champions teach themselves to expect the unexpected and to know how to handle these events calmly. This is how God develops His prophets through experiences and mentorship; this is how we are to develop.

As prophets, we are taught to practice calmness in the presence of God, as we know He has our back. Imagine Moses going to Pharaoh's face knowing how to be calm under the stress of talking to a national leader with the tremendous power of Pharaoh.

And the Lord said to Moses, "When you go back to Egypt, see that you do all those wonders before Pharaoh which I have put in your hand. But I will harden his heart so that he will not let the people go. Then you shall say to Pharaoh, 'Thus says the Lord: "Israel is My son, My firstborn. 23 So I say to you, let My son go that he may serve Me. But if you refuse to let him go, indeed I will kill your son, you're firstborn."— Exodus 4:21-23 (AKJV)

That's what Moses and others faced, but what about us? Prophets, we do have choices:

1. We can stand and proclaim a disaster and ask God why He allowed this to happen to us or
2. We can focus on our self-confidence, and deal with the unexpected challenge and seek God for insight.

So, prophet, how do you want to handle this? It is your call. You can become a championship level prophet or a runner, or a flat-out bum prophet. We all have the choice to make.

There is a connection with sports and the prophetic ministry. We see many of the same tools and principles needed for success. This is not by accident. This is divine intervention. We as the prophets of this generation must be aware and sensitive to the call of God upon our lives and what it means to be successful in this generation.

We are not in the Biblical days, nor do we lack any company as we find ourselves in a time where everyone is a self-help guru on what we need to do next. One thing every prophet needs to realize is that life itself is a championship series of experiences. We don't always come out on top, but we do survive it. The point here is that we get through it.

There are five fundamental points every prophet needs to know about to becoming the 'Championship Prophet of God' and being able to be of service to the people of God. Are you the prophet that will face the challenge, answer to call, and stand his or her ground in the face of overwhelming odds? If you're that prophet, you have these five unique things. If not, write these down so you will not forget.

1. The Prophet's Commitment, Better known as Prophetic Commitment.

This is staying loyal to what you said you were going to do and remaining loyal to what you said God said. Stay loyal to yourself. Commitment is a self-investment that each prophet makes. What hurts most prophets is the dynamics of investment. When we are committed, we see that what we do today, will reflect at a later time. When we invest in anything, you will not see an immediate return. This is why so many prophets quit. They give up because they feel they need to see an immediate return. This is not a championship mentality. This is how the uninformed, uneducated, or non-believer thinks.

Where do you fit in of those categories? Is there something you need to check within yourself? Moses, Abraham, and many other biblical Biblical prophets have given us examples of what it takes to make a committed relationship with God. Are you loyal to God or are you loyal to you?

2. The Prophet's Discipline

What are your goals? What is your focus? You have a choice, prophet, to move forward, or you have a choice to stay where you are. Your goals will drive your choices. There will be a point in your life, where you make a choice that will counter the choices of your peers and your family.

The Prophet's Discipline is saying no to the things that do not move them towards a closer walk with God. The better the prophet is at saying no to the things that keep him or her away from God, the stronger your discipline is as a prophet.

3. The Prophet's Consistency

There is always room in the prophetic for a prophet who is consistent. The consistent prophet is reliable. They do not operate with an on and off switch. One day they are on fire. The next day they are turned off. Many prophets are gifted and anointed, but the ones who God will use are consistent.

They pray, fast, and give. They continuously do 'the small things' every day. They are focused, even when it looks like nothing is happening. They believe in the prophetic process of growth. The element of belief is key here, a, without belief, the prophet will not develop a consistent mentality. Therefore, they are consistent, despite the obstacles.

4. The Prophet's Faith

Believing the odds are beatable, even when you see the odds are impossible. The prophet must believe in the odds that God gave him or her and the vision on what you they are working for. In life, many people will tell you many things about where your faith should be.

What should matter to the prophet is the prophet's relationship with God. Does that relationship reflect confidence in God or, that He is always on your their side? People will laugh, talk about you, and frankly will not believe in you, but you must never lose sight of what God has shown or spoken to you.

One of the hardest things to deal with here is to remove your emotions, so you can discern clearly what God is telling you to do. Your ability to build your faith will come with every test. Everyone, to include family at some time or another, will not see or understand your faith. Don't worry about that, stay connected to your faith in God.

5. The Prophet's Heart

The heart is putting your all into it. When you focus on your all that becomes the norm. There is a reason; that you will not quit. There is a reason that you will not stop. The prophet's mind-set is our most significant limitations. If you know why that is significant, prophet, nothing will stop you.

You as a prophet cannot afford to allow certain mind-sets, to stop your growth. Stop calling itchy ear prophetic whores, itchy ear Christians, or lazy prophetic peers to influence you. If you keep dealing with these types and you will become them and, not know why. They will affect you if you keep dealing with them.

Prophet, you better know where God has called you and who He has called you to. Have you ever seen a prophet, change or become what or who they give access to their life? Why are we dealing with those who bring negativity or constant drama?

CHAPTER 5

The Prophet, Called or Chosen

Over the years, how many times have we heard someone say, "Such and such has been called by the Lord to be a Prophet or a Prophetess?" We all have listened to it. Since many are called (Matthew 22:14) and few are chosen, there is validation to the statement that you are called.

Romans 8:30 says, "Those whom he predestined he also called." He "called "and those whom he called he also justified, and those whom he justified he also glorified."

In Matthew 22:1-14, there is the parable of the wedding feast. A king is giving this feast, and he wants lots of people to come. We all are called, but there is a difference when it comes to an understanding who has been called and called for what and who has been chosen and chosen for what. We need some knowledge and clarity.

To get an understanding, we all must realize some facts of our lives as we live it. Our lives are a moment. One moment, right after the other. These moments represent a series of moments that can change quickly. This is where the difference is between being called or chosen. Let's go more in-depth. God gives us a moment, and what we do in that or any particular moment is a reflection on our gifts from God.

The called will realize the moment, but only the chosen will seize the moment as it belongs to them. When it is your moment, you will see it. Differently, you will realize the gravity of the moment and what needs to be done. Your peers will hesitate, but you will act because God has chosen you for that moment.

As prophets, we should always be grateful for the great moments in our lives. These are the moments that God called us for and chose us individual gifts specifically and especially to perform a specific task.

The chosen prophets are passionate about being called by God. The chosen prophets understand that they own the moment. They know this, they walk in it, and they do not doubt it. The prophets chosen for a particular task are not waiting for your approval, nor are they waiting for your opinion.

The chosen prophet understands that the greatest moments of their life are born in crisis. The crisis in life is the divine creators of a hero. The hero will always see the situation differently. This is not just true in the prophet's life but in all walks of life. The hero will always see it differently.

Prophet, can you imagine waking up one morning and your life is the same, yet it is the time you have been chosen by God for? The day starts as a normal day for you. There is nothing strange or nothing new in your life, but yet you are only moments away from the greatest moment or moments in your life. Are you ready to deal with this?

Many of us miss the most significant moments of our lives. We allow the crisis or the issue to be bigger than God. In doing this, we miss the moment. This is as simple as that; we miss the moment. One prophet who did not miss the moment was David. We can debate on the merit of David being a prophet, or we can look at his life and see the example God shows us in His word about being called and knowing you're chosen.

1 Samuel 17 describes a normal day in David's life. We also see a day that presents a moment in David's life for an opportunity of greatness. This is how David knew this was his moment. He saw it differently. Everyone else was standing and murmuring about the situation with Goliath. David

saw an opportunity for himself, his family, his nation, and, most of all, his God.

Was David special? Well if you call being the black sheep of the family special, he probably was in that aspect. We should also consider that his brothers are not happy with him as he has been prophesied over by Samuel to be the next king.

We see David as an outcast who God has big plans for because he has a relationship with God that he won't deny. David defines the title of a servant as he brings his brother's lunch, and walks into the moment of his Destiny.

Get this, his small assignment was to bring lunch to his half-brothers who did not like or appreciate him (Psalm 51, Psalm 69). David could have had the big head and reminded his father, Jessie, of his future appointment as king, but he did not. He served. He brought lunch, and God gave him his divine glory for his trouble.

David proves that God will bless you for the most important tasks, especially ones that others do not want to do. Every great prophet should respect small assignments. Can you imagine if David would not have taken lunch to his brothers that day? David had a servant's heart. Without a servant's heart, you will miss your moment.

Your pride will be in the way, and you will not be able to see that your moment is before you. You were chosen by God. You missed the moment because you, prophet, allowed your pride to get in the way.

Notice how David tells his brother Eliab in 1 Samuel 17:28-29, "Is there not a cause?" Yes, we are called by God, by our positions, and our status, but we have a real cause, and why don't you see that? David's gift got him in position, but his character kept him informed on how to handle the situation.

This is why the enemy wants to kill the heart of a servant, prophet. The enemy wants you to be and stay bitter and not serve. David had every reason to be bitter and not serve. He could have become bitter from not being among the brothers when Jessie gathered them for Samuel. He could have wondered how Jessie had the gall to ask him to bring food to brothers who did not like or appreciate him.

David served, and he was the only one who saw what God wanted to be done. Many were called that day to gather. But only David, God's prophet, was chosen for the mission. He saw what and who Goliath was. He saw what God wanted to do and was available to do it. He was passionate about it. He knew that was his moment among others who were called, but did not respond to the moment.

Many are called, and few are chosen. Remember, as we are called, we all will have a charge to be utilized by God for a chosen time. God is calling you to the Nations, but unless you prepare, you will never know when your time to go is. How do we know that?

When your time comes, you will present yourself. You will have the foundation of a prophet to the nation in place, so when the opportunity comes, you will see it, know it, and be passionate about it. You will serve to build it.

Therefore, when prophets come and say God sent them here to do such and such, look and observe the fruit they produce. The fruit of God will always reflect the assignment of God. We saw it in the life of David, Abraham, Elijah, Elisha, Deborah, Anna, Moses, and other prophets sent to the nations by God.

Remember that as a prophet, you're gifted to look at the supernatural, the impossible, and even the dead and call for the possibility to manifest. You do not have to know why it is that way. You need to know God, prophet.

There are two very important questions to ask yourself in every situation that you are involved in.

1. How do I see the situation?
2. Do I have the confidence to implement what God is showing me in the situation?

Know that you will and may face opposition. How you handle it will be a determining factor.

Your ability to handle the situation will have a direct effect on who you are and are not in covenant with. When God calls you to your defining moment, prophet, some things will be obvious to you. God's choice will be clear and not debated. Again, notice that David went through every test and, every excuse, not to send him, to include Saul's plea with him, and yet David was up to the challenge.

David knew that despite the challenges he must push through. There is a reason for him to stand even if no one else will stand. Funny how earlier that morning it was a normal day. It turned into a life-defining moment, what God chose him for, and he was ready. Does this sound like your life, prophet?

The moment, you have been chosen for, is directly related to the time you have suffered for. Now your anointing is on display. This is now in your defining moment. Do not lose your moment because you fall out with someone who can provide you the access to the opportunity you need in God for you to move forth.

In other words, relationships are your greatest source of opportunity and who you fall out with may have your transfer. This is what the devil does not want you to get.

Imagine if David had of falling out with his father. He would not have gotten the opportunity to serve and be in position for his defining moment. Our lives are a series of moments. We must know when our moment of defining greatness has come, and take full advantage of it.

Relationships are everything, and we all should strive to build them. We are all candidates for the moments God wants to demonstrate His glory whenever, wherever, and however.

CHAPTER 6

What's your Relationship with Prophetic Money

An undeniable fact of the bible is that there are over 500 verses in the on the subject of prayer, and 2,350 verses about money and material possessions. This is not by accident, either.

Every prophet needs to have not just a clear and solid understanding, but a mature understanding of his or her heart concerning money. This is the one topic you will be judged, examined and securitized for, whether outwardly or inward.

One thing is sure, that is when you will not give to God when He says to give, this should tell you what you think of Him. Forget your emotions because of something you do not like, or someone you do not like. What is God saying? Many of us have a problem with this because we include our emotions and we mix that with God. We are seeing and hearing the wrong way.

This is something too many have done. Too many of us have tried to justify this, but the reality is that your money will be planted where your heart is. Check your resources and then see how it lines up with your love walk with God. This is a sobering thought for all of us.

"No one can serve two masters. Either he will hate the one and love the other, or he will be devoted to the one and despise the other. You cannot serve both God and Money."—Matthew 6:24 (NIV)

Jesus makes it clear that this is impossible, "You cannot serve God and money."

So, let's, look at prophetic money as we check ourselves. Has our faith developed in the Glory realm, so that we can call things into existence that are not available in the natural realm as we look and work with our natural senses?

This is the definition and birth of prophetic money. The prophet of God is calling finances and, resources in from all directions. The accumulation of wealth, the maintaining of health, and the foundation of prophetic words that activate what we do and see into the now generation revelation. The prophetic gift is establishing prosperity in the life of ones who will receive that right now!

Make no mistake; the warfare to this is great. The enemy had lined up forces and fortified them within the Body of Christ on this topic. The enemy agents are against the prosperity of the people of God, so they have referred to the prophet as money hungry, clowns of the Gospel, and hustlers.

These are just a few of the names, and shameful titles given to prophets, but they will ignore the fundraising activities for unscriptural events such as a pastor's birthday or anniversary. We are to honor the servants of God, but warfare is waged on the prophetic mantle, even for a trained and mature prophet, in the areas of finances and resources. In 1 Timothy 5:17-18, "Those who provide effective leadership must be counted worthy of double honor, especially those who work hard in speaking and teaching." For the scripture says, "Do not muzzle an ox while it is treading out the grain," and, "The worker deserves his pay."

Everyone should continue to honor their man or woman of God, but you should also make sure you are in tune to the move of God when He wants seed planted into the mantle of one or more of His prophetic voices. The reality is that the prophet of God is a worker, As hard as the job is, they must be attentive to God, regardless of how you or anyone may feel about a prophet.

Unbelief, anger, and a lack of understanding of who the prophet of God is has stopped and stranded prophets and people in general in the body of Christ, from getting prophetic money. Unbelief will put a stop on a prophetic word in your life from a prophet of God.

God has shown us there have been far too many testimonies of blessings of prophetic money. These miracles of prophetic money happen in the lives of people who can process the faith to seed into the supernatural. This is what was not there, but the money that showed up because they seeded into the mantle or gift that God was using to speak upon the sowers.

Yes, even the most traditional haters of the prophetic gift, will have to turn their heads and act like they don't see the blessings of God. The people who sowed into the mantle of prosperity received the blessings of prophetic money.

Others will ignore or belittle it. Do not worry about them; keep going forth in faith.

2 Chronicles 20:20 says, "Believe in His word so shall we be established; believe His prophet so shall you prosper." This was a word not for your entrainment, but for your establishment of prosperity. We see the enemy immediately going on assignment to try to stop the word of God on finances, especially. The key to the release is not just a hit and miss. It is laboring and growing in the time as well as the timing of God for the season you're in.

The birthing of prophetic money, from people who make pledges or commitments, many times becomes victims of the poverty theology of the Body of Christ. This type of theology has ruled the Body of Christ on financial matters for years.

This theology works off our lack of understanding the word of God on the subject of lack and the poor. This theology specializes in making us feel bad and out of touch with God if we have material things. This way of thinking feeds our undeveloped habits of giving. Say Amen! It is true.

This is why we will not sow. This is why we constantly come up with reasons not to do this and not to do that. Have you ever noticed how people change when challenges come into their life, especially in the way of finances?

Prophetic money starts in the faith of the individual, not in a local bank account. The release of a prophet on the subject is very personal. It is dependent on your obedience and the timing of God. Many prophets get frustrated because of the timing of the release of this prophetic money. Please understand that it starts in the faith realm.

We can't expect a harvest in our lives, and we have planted no seed. This is a grave error that is alive and well in the body of Christ today. This is what too many depend on. They want and expect a harvest, just because they showed up.

Prophets should be the first sowers. Prophet, your job as a sower is to make sure the seed is planted, and the Word is spread. Prophets of God are called to plants seeds. We must understand that God may never allow us to see the harvest of what we've planted, but, if we don't plant the seeds, there won't be a harvest.

Prophets, we are called to plants seeds of encouragement in the lives of everyone we touch; our children, grandchildren, coworkers, neighbors, the people in the seats next to you, in front, and behind you. Prophet, you must understand we are called to plant seeds of encouragement for the Kingdom of God, through other prophets, who are your peers.

Seed sowing is a product of prophetic money, and for us to sow seed is supposed to be the lifestyle of all believers, including the prophets. God does not intend that you sow seeds occasionally. You will end up as a spiritual beggar, digger, or a sower in life. Renew your mind on God's plan for your prosperity.

Prophetic money also exposes one to the key realities of the toiling side of life. God never intended that you live out of toilsome labor, but out of the harvest of the seed sown. This is why constituency opens us a portal of divine communication with a prophet, which is available nowhere else.

The most important point for you to realize is that prophetic money will not work for you prophet until you realize that you need a harvest more than God needs your seed. God is the owner of the cattle upon a thousand hills, and if He was hungry, or needed something, He already has it.

Prophet, anytime you're asked to sow a seed into the life of your man of God, the house of God, or the work of God, let these words always ring in your heart and in your mind, "I need my harvest more than God needs the seed."

Too many prophets blow the opportunity to sow seeds and gain access to the portal of blessings because they are looking at the individual and not at the God of the individual. The process of sowing seeds of prayer, seeds of the right words, seeds of time, and seeds of money is priceless because there is a harvest that is already awaiting the seed you are asked to sow. If you sow with a cup, God will give you a cupful of harvest, but God's cup is always bigger than your cup. Prophet, please get this revelation and allow God to bless you.

How many prophets do you know are a victim of not understanding prophetic money? We see this prophet does not give, period. No, it is not that many prophets don't give because they don't have. Far too many prophets, and people of God, simply never intend to give, because of how they understand the theology of poverty in the Body of Christ. Ecclesiastics 7:12 says money is a defense. That means it is a connector. It will connect us to the anointing of prosperity. Why do you think the enemy fights the prophet so hard in this area?

Our inability, or refusal, lack of attention, or our distorted view of money in the Body of Christ someone will prioritize one gifting over another and seemly cram that down our throat, has intimidated us on fully educating ourselves in the area of finances in the kingdom of God. Combine this with the fact that we see the enemy change people and go to great lengths to destroy the carriers of the anointing of prosperity or the prophets of God.

Prophets, like many people in the body of Christ, will always rationalize that what they have is hardly enough for themselves. So how can they be expected to sow seeds? The understanding of how to turn not enough into a seed builds the faith for prophetic money (Philip. 4:17). Ask yourself, "Is your harvest in the order of God?" By not planting, you get nothing. But in the kingdom of God, there is a guaranteed return.

You're a prophet, God's prophet. You're an oracle of prosperity, and God is not unjust as to forget your labor of love. He will not ask you for seed without the intention of giving you a bountiful harvest.

You need to sow a seed to activate your prophetic money. So many prophets and people of God have lost great harvests simply because they never knew that their harvest came ahead of the seed. Remember, He is God. He already has your harvest!

When there is a money anointing or/ prosperity anointing upon a prophet, you can either trust God's word on it or do it your way. Prophetic money activates the seed. Sow your seed as you stake your claim to the prophetic word. Then you will place yourself in a position to receive the blessings of God. The reality is our way has not worked. We need God's miracle-working prophetic money.

When we allow the process to move forth, we then allow for stewardship to take place. Stewardship shows us what our relationship to material possessions is supposed to be. It is not poverty. It's the balance between poverty and prosperity that keeps us focused on God.

Stewardship is the watchman that sees the deceitfulness of wealth. The desires for other things come in and choke the word, making it unfruitful. Stewardship keeps us properly balanced, then the wealth will not be deceitful wealth, the money is really a defense and that connects you to the anointing.

My prophetic friend, I curse the fear that is keeping you from accumulating and activating prophetic money in your lives. You will become fruitful. Nothing is wrong with Godly accumulation. Stewardship is the enemy of idolatry. Idolatry is always a matter of the heart. The truth is that we begin to understand that material goods, that house, and everything you have, is not your own.

7 IMPORTANT RULES EVERY PROPHET SHOULD KNOW ABOUT WEALTH

Have you ever wondered what is holding us back in the Body of Christ, from having the financial success we need in the body of Christ? Many books have been written on the subject, and many teachings are available also. Before we discuss seven important rules every prophet should know about wealth and money, we need to consider two simple things in the area of wealth and money management. Those things are:

1. Belief

With no belief, how can there be any faith? There will be no hope much less the evidence of the unseen miracle-working power of God. Most prophets never realize they are living and participating in the world of doubt and disbelief. In the arena of finances, this is on full display.

2. Most importantly our relationship with God.

We can confess all day and never display, much less execute, positive action in our relationship with God. In other words, our confession is not backed with action. Faith without works is just as dead as our relationship with God. In the arena of finances, our relationship with prophetic money is nonexistence.

We also need to define wealth and money separately, so we clearly understand God's plan and purpose for both. Our money is a currency, which is a type or form of wealth. Our wealth is our accumulated resources that hold value. Keep in mind our wealth is not always necessarily money.

Our wealth can come in many forms other than material possessions. Have you ever noticed what the world tells us about money? Things like have a plan, spend less, invest, and get out of debt. All these things are all good things, but the kingdom has some rules we need to apply for which is the greatest investment, we will ever make.

To the prophets who are ready for change, we must realize that there is some work to be done in our lives in this area. To the prophets, who feel they have arrived or at least know everything they need to know, this will only make them yawn. Most of you, who are wealthy, are still searching, for something that seems to be hidden from you. Jesus said that I have come that you would have life and life more abundantly. We serve a God of addition. We do not serve a God of less than enough!

Allow me to present seven rules every prophet of God should be aware of so that he or she will, at a minimum, establish a foundation of wealth establishment in his or her life.

1. Wealth is attracted to the prophet you become.

We must become more skilled in our prophetic gifts for Gods work. We must understand that to walk in a greater anointing opens the door for the changes that should be made in our individual lives. Your level of wealth as a prophet can never surpass your level of personal development as a prophet.

The prophet Jonah was sent to Nineveh, and in the situation, he was in, he failed to grow because he did not want to do what God had called him to do. He could not become the prophet God called him to be, because of his prejudices and attitude towards the Gentiles. Read the entire book of Jonah.

The opportunities for wealth are attracted to the prophet we have become. This is why we need to keep growing. Prophets of God should always look for the opportunities within the kingdom, in other words, we must have a desire before we can acquire. Embrace the opportunities God gives us. Remember, we only get these opportunities when we prove to God, He can trust us. Therefore, we need to work hard on our prophetic gifts and skills.

2. Understand that money, or currency flows, and this means ours.

Your money needs to be active. Prophets are to actively spend and invest in the kingdom of God. When our money is not flowing, it is not going somewhere. Someone is benefitting from our money. Our money needs to move within the kingdom of God.

We actively do this by tithing, sowing seeds, offerings, and investing in ministry visions through visionaries. A currency that does not flow becomes a deterrent to the purposes of God's through His visionaries. Why the prophets of today do not believe in sowing into an anointing? Too many of our prophetic peers have no problem receiving, but we do have a problem giving.

This has to be tangible proof, or we simply will not believe. The Kingdom of God is the greatest investment we can make. Ecclesiastes 7:12 says,

"Money is a defense, (a shadow, a covering) that works hand in hand with wisdom." We are saying this can't be true, when we look at our actions, because the excellency of knowledge is that wisdom that giveth light to them that have it. We are saying to God that we reject His wisdom and we know better how to handle our troubles better.

3. Wealth nor money is a friend of complainers.

You're a prophet, and your words have power. You're always talking about what you don't have, speaking evil, and distressing things on the wealth anointing, on someone's life, rest assured you will never have any wealth. Wealth and money both hate complainers; both will search to find prophets, who use words build wealth. We have a responsibility to learn about the wealth anointing. We are to stop cursing ourselves and our generational lineage especially when we are speaking about money.

As prophets, we need to stop cursing wealth and wealthy people. We are saying we don't want wealth or money nor is it of God. That is a lie. Have you ever seen people who speak and condemn prophets and other people when money is involved, but it's okay when it is their pastor?

"Is the servant of God double worthy?" (1 Timothy 5:17) Prophets, so many times prophets are excluded from the title of a servant of God when money and wealth are the issue of the discussion. We so often are referred to a money hungry, greedy, and robber of the saints.

We have demonic activity in all areas of society on, all levels. We need to be careful how we put our mouth on a real prophet of God. Did you know that 1 Samuel 9:7 tells us that we are not to come before a prophet without a gift in our hands. This is the only gift in the five-fold this is spoken of in this manner, and you wonder why we have the stigma of people bad mouthing us about money.

4. Wealth and money love hard workers who create value for our society.

Prophet, your anointing and, your gift are important to society in, this generation. You have suffered for your anointing, and through your hard work, you have created much value to society. Your gift has now positioned itself to be sought, and you're rewarded as you honor the gift God has given you. God now puts you on a full-time platform for His Glory because He trusts your work ethic and is pleased with the value, you create.

Your value is reflected in your hard work and service to your fellow man. The prophet needs to realize that we all are equal in the sight of God. Mature prophets will reach this place. Look at the life of Moses, Joseph, Samuel, Elijah, Elisha, and Anna. All mature prophets of God understand hard work. This is the foundation of how God creates value through your gift.

5. Your wealth or money needs protection. You must watch it.

Wealth must be disciplined by the holder of the money. Too many times, wealth and money tell us what to do because we have not become educated upon it. We can't protect what we don't know needs protection.

Wealth and money should not tell us what to do. Prophets, we are to tell it what to do. Too many times we have money and then it is gone. We can't account for it. Our money cannot any longer disrespect us. We are the visionaries who God has called in this generation to create, maintain and sustain platforms for his His Glory.

6. Move your emotions out of your money; you will never build wealth.

In the Body of Christ, we make so many emotional decisions, which are not in line with God's principles. Our emotions become the logic for our decisions. The reality is that our emotions must not be the main decision made in our monetary transaction process. We have to put away our personal preferences and listen to God. We have to stop hiding behind our emotional insecurity and deep-seated emotional prejudices. We are quick to say its God.

We know when we say it's God, people will back off and not challenge, so this becomes our safety valve to allow our emotions to rule our life and our money. Many of us have brought, done things emotionally, not sowed, and made excuses. We use a different type of logic in worldly issues, which never seems to flow with the Church. Our emotions will always talk us into letting someone else give it, especially when God has told us to offer and we do not want to.

7. Wealth and money are available to every believer, and, yes, every prophet.

The ability to get money is like sunshine. The sunshine is for everyone. The sunshine, rain, and the weather do not discriminate against anyone. Prophets of God have to figure out how to find the opportunities in God; will lead us to our wealth.

Prophets are responsible for this, not anyone else. Look closer at 2 Chronicles 20:20 "Believe in the word of God, so shall you be established, believe in his prophet so shall you prosper." Nowhere does it say that if you are a certain ethnic group, or if you are of a certain faith.

There is no statute that says, "because you had a bad experience in ministry or church," this is not applying to you! Oh, so wrong! Look at the keyword here again: "Believe!" You and I are told to believe. The reason so many of us are not having success in this area is our abundance of "hidden unbelief."

Let's get real. The fact that prophets and people of God resent giving shows the condition of their hearts. Our giving should be a 'thank you' offering to God. Giving is for believers, and it should be done by all believers. Giving is for all prophets, poor prophets, and wealthy prophets, should give to the Lord (2 Cor. 8:2; Luke 21:1-4).

Every prophet must come to understand that giving is not just about "doing their duty." Giving is the self-indicator of our spiritual maturity as well as our love for God. As prophets, we know that the word "treasure" is an indication of our "heart." We must empower and educate others on the importance of giving.

CHAPTER 7

The Investment of a Prophet's Friend

Who are your friends? The life of a prophet is lonely, and many times marked with trails of deceitfulness. For prophets, a true friend should help strengthen your Biblical values. Proverbs 27:17 explains it this way, "As iron sharpens iron, so one man sharpens another." But the Word also warns that "bad company corrupts good character" (1 Corinthians 15:33).

We want to choose friends who will sharpen us, not corrupt us (Proverbs 27:5–6). A friend won't tell us what we want to hear, but what we need to hear. "Better is open rebuke than hidden love. Faithful are the wounds of a friend; profuse or deceitful are the kisses of an enemy."

A true friend in the prophetic ministry will put enough trust in you to tell you openly of your faults. The reality is that prophets all hunger for a prophetic friend who will speak honestly to them face to face and instead of not telling others. They will stand on the principle that I am your prophetic brother or sister and, I must tell you directly.

That's a true prophetic friend. But the reality is we never get any praise for telling people of their faults. Too many of us, today confuse friendship with flattery. Sometimes people will say what you want to hear because they do not think you're valuable enough to them to tell you what you need to hear.

Friendship in ministry and the prophetic is an investment that says I'm willing to face your wrath and anger even if it appears as an enemy to get you to be blessed in the long run. The investment of friendship transcends, builds, and separates trust from flattery. Being a friend means I'm committed to you for your walk in your destiny.

Do you ever notice how people, who may not like you, say things you may want to hear, and those who like you say things you don't like? This is why the kisses of an enemy are deceitful. Faithful are the wounds of a friend. You can be kissed and hated at the same time. Therefore, your relationship with God is the key to unlock the Judas in your life.

How many of us have missed the opportunity to have God as a friend? A God that will walk with you, talk with you, tell, and share with you. The kind of God that tells you you're making a mistake, the kind of God that will tell you to trust the process. This is the kind of God who will be intimately associated with you, your failures, and your dysfunctions.

Remember, Judas kissed Jesus and he was not a friend. He was an enemy. Jesus was known as a "friend of sinners (Luke 7:34)." and He has promised, "Never will I leave you; never will I forsake you (Hebrews 13:5)." Jesus is truly the friend who sticks closer than a brother, and blessed are those who have Him as their friend (John 15:14)."

You need prophetic discernment to help you figure out who to deal with and who not to deal with. Discernment will help you receive things that hurt you and helps you process flattery. The anointing of discernment will identify who is who in your life.

As a prophet, you need to know who your friends are. Too many of the prophets today are operating in dysfunction. We are running from God. Instead of running to God, we are running for the cheers, at-a-boys, and the companionship, but not the covenant. Compliments that flatter us or give us a false sense of reality are not helpful.

Proverbs 18:24 (NIV) teaches, "One who has unreliable friends or companions soon comes to ruin, but there is a friend who sticks closer than a brother." Given the fact that we normally think of blood being thicker than water, this proverb is hard hitting and real.

A prophet with many friends may still run into problems. Many friends do not equally help in the time of need. The genuine or authentic friend is someone who sticks closer than a brother; he or she can be counted on. This friend is steadfast; he or she will be there for you even more so than a family member. A friend who sticks closer than a brother is a trustworthy friend, indeed.

The sad reality is that social media promotes many superficial connections who are called "friends," but they are no more than companions rather than true friends. Even the most connected can be lonely. Do you remember the song? "What a friend we have in Jesus, all our sins and griefs to bear?" There is a friend who sticks closer than a brother."

The concept of friendship is a strong one in Proverbs, and the word friend is used multiple times to illustrate the importance of friendship. Wisdom is called a friend (Proverbs 7:4). A friend loves at all times (Proverbs 17:17). A poor man is deserted by his friend (Proverbs 19:4). Everyone is a friend to a man who gives gifts (Proverbs 19:6). A person with gracious speech has the king as his friend (Proverbs 22:11). Faithful are the wounds of a friend (Proverbs 27:6). The sweetness of a friend comes from his earnest counsel (Proverbs 27: 9). Do not forsake your friend and father's friend (Proverbs 27:10).

The question to ponder is are you struggling with rejection from family or friends? Sometimes we trust the wrong people, and we get hurt. Have you ever trusted the wrong person? It's a disaster. It hurts you, and you start cutting people off your list. You become like Jacob, left alone with God.

How does Jacob end up alone? How do we as prophets sometimes end up alone? We focus on the struggle instead of the struggle of being left alone, with no friends, no resources, or no place? People see you and your struggle with your issues.

Jacob's life was one of the never-ending struggles, despite his multiple wives, concubines, land, and possessions. Though God promised Jacob that through him would not only come a great nation but a whole company of nations, he was a man full of fears and anxieties. And now he is about to meet his brother, Esau, who has vowed to kill him. All of Jacob's struggles and fears are about to be realized.

Sick of his father-in-law's treatment, Jacob has fled Laban, only to encounter his embittered brother, Esau. Anxious for his very life, Jacob concocted a bribe and sent a caravan of gifts along with his women and children across the River Jabbok in hopes of pacifying his brother.

Now physically exhausted, alone in the desert wilderness, facing sure death, he's divested of all his worldly possessions. He's powerless to control his fate. He collapses into a deep sleep on the banks of the Jabbok River. With his father-in-law behind him and Esau before him, he was too spent to struggle any longer.

Jacob needs a friend in this time of struggle in his life. Now he is wrestling with God as an angelic stranger visited Jacob. They wrestled throughout the night until daybreak, at which point the stranger that crippled Jacob with a blow to his hip that disabled him with a limp for the rest of his life. It was by then Jacob knew what happened. "I saw God face to face, and yet my life was spared (Genesis 32:30)." In the process, Jacob the deceiver received a new name, Israel, which likely means "He struggles with God." However, what is most important occurs at the conclusion of that struggle. We read that God "blessed him there (Genesis 32:29)."

God was a friend to Jacob despite his favoritism towards his son, Joseph, caused a great rift of hatred in his other sons. His family suffered through Rachel's death in childbirth, Reuben's treachery of sleeping with his concubine, Simeon and Levi's bloodthirsty murders of a whole city in retribution for their sister's rape, and severe famine. As an elderly man, Jacob was eventually reunited with Joseph, and he worshipped God.

Just like Jacob, every prophet will have some type of failure, and we can't go back and change it. We must go forward in the hope that the Lord will turn our failures for our good. Paul wrote in Philippians 3:13-14, "Forgetting what is behind and straining toward what is ahead, I press on toward the goal to win the prize for which God has called me heavenward in Christ Jesus." We have hope in Christ that our sins are completely forgiven even though we may have to deal with the consequences.

As prophets, we must know who is, in our lives and who is willing to make the investment in our lives and allow us due to reciprocity. A true prophetic friend is someone who is trustworthy. You've got to be able to live up to your word and keep a confidence. Are you "using" someone as a friend until a better option comes along? A true friend would never do that. True friendship finds fulfillment in encouraging, supporting, and building up the other person. A real friend is always faithful and looking to protect and seek what's best for the other person.

A true prophetic friend is genuine. Telling your friends what they mean to you, find ways of expressing affection that is genuinely your style. Realizing no one ever gets tired of hearing that he or she is loved, valued, and appreciated. The important part is being consistent and making sure your thoughts are communicated and received.

A true prophetic friend is always honest. Friendship is a process. Do not share the most intimate details of your life until your friends have proven that they will love you and value what you share. Their ability to be respectful means listening without interrupting.

It means you don't focus on your friends' weaknesses but look at their strengths. It means avoiding a judgmental (condemning) and critical spirit. Your friends should walk away from you feeling they've been treated as the most important people in the world.

A true prophetic friend is always a servant. We see that selfishness is one of the biggest enemies of true friendship. Rather than asking what your friend can do for you, find what you can do for them. Make a deliberate effort to discover what your friend needs. Kind words? A helping hand? Encouragement? Comfort? One of the side benefits of serving your friends in this manner is that, often, they will respond by returning the favor.

As long as you're speaking the truth in love, tough times can prove to be foundation blocks in your relationship (Proverbs 9:8). If you ignore every wrongdoing and bottle up all the hurt inside, you will grow increasingly angry and probably wind up lashing out under pressure — something that almost always proves damaging to friendship.

The friendship between Jonathan and David developed into fast friends following the battle in which David killed Goliath. Despite the many hardships both men faced, they remained faithful to one another as friends and protected one another from harm. Jonathan even risked his life interceding for David before King Saul, who sought to kill David. After Jonathan's death, David wrote a lament for his friend, "Jonathan lies slain on your heights. I grieve for you, Jonathan my brother; you were very dear to me (2 Samuel 1:25–26)." Their friendship was stronger than David's relationship with any of his own brothers.

Jesus had 12 disciples. His inner circle — His closest friends — were there in number: Peter, James, and John. No doubt, they laughed and had fun together while they learned about God and trained for their mission. If even Jesus considers friendship of great value, how much more do the rest of us need close friends?

Relationships are difficult to maintain in the best of circumstances. Sometimes family and friends break up over the smallest events, and we are left to pick up the pieces of brokenness. In Romans 12:18 we learn that, "if it is possible, as far as it depends on you, live at peace with everyone." We can't control the actions, thoughts, or decisions of other people, but we can control our response to them with the love and care of Christ Jesus.

Every believer will have struggling moments with God. We are finite creatures, and He is an infinite, all-knowing God and Father of heaven. While the Lord orchestrates the joy and sorrow of our lives, we must continually trust Him through the difficult days. We struggle with our faith in God, and we need to "know that the testing of your faith produces perseverance...let perseverance finish its work so that you may be mature and complete, not lacking anything (James 1:3-4)." Our struggle with God is necessary for us to prove our confidence in Him.

CHAPTER 8

Prophets & The Blessings of the Good-bye Gift

As a prophet, do you know how many covenant friends you have? The definition of a good friend varies from person to person, but there are certain traits, characteristics, and qualities that most prophets would agree that makes someone a covenant friend."

For many prophets going through the process of becoming who God mandated them to be will deal with various issues. One of the hardest things to do is understand why people and even prophets walk out of your life, many times with no explanation at all. The prophet thinks, "Did I do something? It doesn't make any sense; we were fine before! Nothing happened, and we didn't fight! So why is this happening? How many times has that happened to you?

Prophets, as gifted as we are, can be very immature in the way that we deal with things. Sometimes we are stressed out with other things going on in our life; we may decide to take it out on those who are supposed to be close to us. The reality is this is a personal issue in each person or each prophet's life.

When a prophet or a person walks away out of your life, the most important thing for you as a prophet to understand is that your destiny is not tied to people who have left you or walked out of your life.

They have left, your life, and the reality is that they are not tied to you, nor do they want to be connected to you. You're strong enough to walk out of my life, and then I must be strong enough to understand that my destiny is not tied or connected to you. This must especially include people who want to walk in and out of your life like a movie theater. Again, they are not a part of your destiny, and you must realize it sooner, than later.

They went out from us, but they were not of us; for if they had been of us, they would no doubt have continued with us: but they went out, that they might be made manifest that they were not all of us. —(1 John 2:19)

The comfort in understanding the irrational behavior of your prophetic peers, your supposed friends in life, and the prophetic, is illustrated in 1 John 2:19.

Every now generation prophet or prophetic person needs to understand the different types of people God, allows in your life, constituents, comrades, and covenant people. Constituents are simply people and prophets, who we are connected to by gifts, beliefs, customs as well as traditions. These are people that we are grouped with for basically common reasons. They know each other but are not necessary friends. We see an abundance of this today.

Comrades are people and prophets who are on your side. They will always be your friends and side by side with you as long as you both have a common enemy or a common cause. This relationship is not based on any other foundation except that of commonality. This relationship can mature into a covenant relationship once each party understands its responsibilities.

Prophets the bottom line is if someone doesn't see the value of your friendship or the value of your relationship, they don't deserve you. Real friends don't leave when life gets rough. , They stick by you, and when you may disagree, they will work things out with you. No real friend or a real relationship will just leave when they feel like it. It does not matter if they're just "stressed out." They fail to see the relationship is a dual responsibility issue.

Real prophetic friendship is a covenant relationship. Real friends are so hard to find nowadays. People come and go for a season or a reason. It will make your life better if you understand you need to forgive and forget to be able to move on with your life. This is easier said than done. Not everyone is meant to stay in your life, and not everyone is worth keeping in your life either.

The prophets and the others, who walk out of your life, never did matter in your picture of your self-worth to them as a true friend. Prophets, we must understand that we can identify our true friends that help guide and support you us in everything that we do, rather than the ones who abandon us and or tear us down. Consider this real talk.

Once someone walks out of your life, you might feel unimportant, but you shouldn't. When people walk out of your life, it shows they are in the mind-set of not caring about you and maybe never did. Who wants someone like that, in their life as you realize who they are? Prophets do not lower your standards.

We learn another valuable and a hard lesson as we study the life of David. Death is impactful in the arena of learning how to deal with loss of people in one's life. Here is a key to developing the 'Gift of Good bye.' Once David lost his 1st first son that he had with Bathsheba in 2 Samuel 12, he rose up with all his pain and grief. He, washed his face, bathed, prayed, and accepted it as the will of God and then made another baby with Bathsheba.

David showed every prophet that God is faithful. Anyone who you lose in your life was not part of the will of God for your life, in the next season of your life. Prophets, if God gives us what we need, then people who are strong enough to walk away from our lives for whatever reason, should be let go. Wave and let them go.

The simple fact is they do not know who you are, no matter how much they may say they do. Prophets must get to the point that they understand some of the people, and prophetic peers who were supposed to stay close to you, will walk out of your life. Your reality is that they don't understand what you carry.

They have seen your gift, and make an assumption of your gift based on what they see, not what God says. They act like God is wasting their time as they were your friend or connected to you. They now treat you like you're common or, you're nothing. God lets you see this, so you will see their character and who they are at this time in their life. This is the blessings of the Gift of Goodbye. Those leaving your life revealed some things God wanted you to see about you and life itself.

Character is always exposed in the way people treat people, especially when they feel the person is of no use to them. Prophets do prophets like this, as well as people in the body of Christ, all the time. When you as a prophet see someone walk out of your life, and they let you know they don't need you in how they conducted the split, you will see the true character you were connected to, and your Blessing as the Gift of Good bye is activated.

The Gift of Goodbye shows you that God loves you too much to allow this type of person or this type of prophet to be connected to your life in this next season, or this next move of God. The reality of being a prophet is that as God elevates you in your gift; your circles will be more clearly defined. You need not worry about the size of the circles, as the anointing of the circle you are now placed in is more important than anything else in your life.

The reality of real friends in a prophet's life is important for empowerment. The Elijah and Elisha relationship is a classic standard of covenant and empowerment. Even during the tough times, neither of them walked out on the other. They demonstrated there is a way to do anything, even when you disagree.

Sometimes prophets can be connected and have friends that lead you into sin, as we see as Jonadab persuades Amnon to rape his half-sister, Tamar (2 Samuel 13:1-6). Even if our friends do not lead us astray, they can provide false comfort or bad advice. The friends of Job, just like the friends of a prophet, can impact and make the suffering worse and displeasing the Lord (Job 2:11-13, 6:14-27, 42:7-9).

Prophets must also be aware of friends that provide false love such as, pretending to give affection for their motives and deserting us when our friendship no longer benefits them (Psalm 55:12-14; Proverbs 19:4, 6-7). Notice I will never tell you this is right, but I will tell you God will teach and train you during the brief time these people and prophets are connected to your life.

Many 'Prophetic Friendships' have been broken through channels of unproven and immature gossip (Proverbs 16:28) or even grudges (Proverbs 17:9). The Apostle Paul taught us that friends should be chosen carefully as "Bad company corrupts good character" (1 Corinthians 15:33).

As prophets, we got to know that the higher we go, the greater God blesses our work for Him. He will only allow those in our life to climb with us that can function in the arena we are promoted to. The thing we should know is that air is thinner the higher we go up, and that means that God is not allowing dead friends, unfaithful friends, backstabbing friends, or copy-cat friends to soar with us in this arena.

So, when they walk away, wave Goodbye. The gift again exposes you to the greatness and the joy of the Lord. Don't even speculate on those who left. All you know is they left and their season in your life was and is over. Stop trying to revive what is dead. Unless the Lord wants it revived, it will never be again.

Perhaps you're one of those prophets who are frustrated today. Understand that frustration is an enemy to the prophetic ministry. People walking in and out of your life can be frustrating. That's why it will always color cloud our thinking, infect the word we have, and give us an unclear perspective on people, other prophets and the living church.

Our job is to represent God's heart and be good servants. We must learn to master our frustration, even when people and or prophets seem to want to do their best to add or create frustration in our lives. God has too much work for you to do to be frustrated on immature, uneducated peers who are not anointed to do what God has called you to do.

It is no secret that prophets and prophetic people seem to have more disappointment than the average person. Prophets will often see clearly how things should be or how God plans for them to be. Proverbs 13:12 says, "Hope deferred makes the heart sick." Because their expectations are typically higher, they are more deeply disappointed.

Did you notice that every time Jeremiah opened his mouth, he got in trouble? The establishment of the day had no tolerance for the young prophet of God, who spoke against them. He was perplexed and, he was ridiculed. He wanted to quit. The issue is that you could count his real friends on one hand and still have several fingers left.

Oh yes, no doubt, the word of the Lord was like a fire burning within Jeremiah, and he could not hold it back (Jeremiah 20:9). Have you ever wondered how many people walked out of his life, outside of his family, who seemed to have trouble with him and his calling? How about Moses? I wonder how many people followed him and yet would not throw urine on his guts if they were on fire! Welcome to real life leadership.

Prophets we all must realize that there is pain that comes with this calling. While some of us will go to great lengths to escape it. The reality is simple and direct. People, who walk out of your life, help you to understand the following seven points every prophet should know and practice in his or her life.

1. Look at them and simply wave goodbye to them.

2. Do not gossip about them.

3. Understand you've positioned you for greater and expect it.

4. Your discernment is sharper as you see character exposed.

5. You have taken a giant step to your destiny.

6. Thank God for the removal of the Unknown burden.

7. Understand 1 John 2:19 "They went out from us, but they were not of us; for if they

had been of us, they would no doubt have continued with us: but they went out, that they might be made manifest that they were not all of us."

This scripture should always bring you comfort in understanding the irrational behavior of your prophetic peers and your supposed friends in life and the prophetic.

Final Thought

There is much more to share but let me suggest that you invest into your life and show up at a School of the Prophets, or the next prophetic training. Sure, I would love for you to show up for our "Where Eagles Fly School," if not show up where there is a prophetic watering. We all need this.

So much of this gift is getting to know who you are and what God has for you. The uncommon edge you will feel is real, as the uncommon quickly becomes your reality. Welcome to your new norm. You're a prophet called of God and you are called to this moment. You are a "Prophet in the moment."

Read and reread this book. Meditate over the concepts and watch your life improve as you become a more effective prophet of God. It is my prayer that God uses you mighty and we get an opportunity to fellowship together and work the work of God. The prophets need each other, as we grow and mature for the supernatural work ahead. Please feel free to contact my office @ 919-695-3375 for information.

Apostle Ken Cox

About The Author

Apostle Ken Cox is a born-again believer, he is a prophet of God who fathers' prophets of all races around the world. Apostle Cox along with his wife, Prophetess Sabina Cox are the leaders of Where Eagles Fly, an international growing prophetic fellowship that is actively working with prophets to go to the Nations. Apostle Cox is the founder of The Prophets Teaching Group on Facebook and has a 1000 plus member following on Periscope TV.

Apostle Cox currently broadcasts on Roku TV, Apple TV, Amazon TV and Android TV along with Prophetess Cox 24 hours a day, 7 Days a week. To Contact Apostle Cox call Where Eagles Fly at 919-695-3375

Index

A

accusations, 11
adversity, 40
agreement, 33
anger, 1, 63, 84
anniversary, 62
anointing, 26, 35–36, 70, 74–75, 77–78, 102
arena, 72, 100, 103

B

battle, 22–24, 92
believers, 66, 80–81, 93
blessings, 30, 67, 95, 101
blood, 26, 86

C

Comfort, 35, 92
conflict, 18, 25
connections, 86
covenant, 8, 57, 85, 102

currency, 72, 75

D

destiny, 31, 34–37, 84, 96–97, 106
disaster, 13, 42
discernment, 85, 106
divine glory, 53
dysfunctions, 84–85

E

emotions, 46, 60, 79–80
enemy, 18, 31, 33–34, 64, 84, 91, 104
establishment, 7, 64

F

failures, 34, 84, 90
faith, 26, 46–47, 63–65, 72, 80, 94
foundation, 9, 55, 61, 73, 98

G

gifts, 10, 30–31, 33, 37, 50–51, 63, 77–78, 88, 98, 101–2

Glory, 2–3, 79
God, 2–4, 6–8, 10–11, 13, 20–23, 25–26, 30–34, 37, 42–47, 50–57, 60–70, 72–81, 84–85, 100–104, 109–10
growth, 8, 15, 35–36

H

harvest, 65–69
history, 36–37
honor, 25, 62, 78

I

idolatry, 71
integrity, 6, 8–13
investment, 7, 44, 82, 90

J

Jeremiah, 6, 105
Jezreelites, 19

K

kingdom, 7, 73–74

kingdom of God, 66, 68–69, 75

L

love, 61, 69, 81, 91–93, 108
loyal, 44

M

manifest, 56, 97, 107
mantle, 18, 27, 34, 63
maturity, 15, 30, 40
mentor, 8–9
ministry, 84

N

nations, 55–56, 88, 110

P

pain, 18, 106
peers, 6, 9, 40, 45, 50, 66
perseverance, 94
personal development, 74
power, 19, 29, 42, 76

prayer, 59, 67
pressure, 19, 92
pride, 54
prophet, 10, 14–15, 49, 54, 64, 82
prophetic, 39, 84, 97, 107
prophetic destiny, 17
prophetic mantle, 8, 62
prophetic ministry, 1, 13, 83, 104
prophetic money, 59, 63, 65–67, 72
prophetic mouthpiece, 15
prophetic peers, 6, 9, 97, 100, 107
prophetic ranks, 5
prophetic subculture, 3
prophetic watering, 108
prophetic words, 28, 61, 63
prosperity, 63–64, 66, 68–69
protection, 78

R

rape, 102
resources, 60–61, 72, 87
retribution, 89
righteousness, 12

S

seeds, 66–67
selfishness, 91
sensitivity, 3
servants, 34, 37, 53, 62, 77, 91, 104
shaken, 32
society, 2, 77–78
soul, 9, 11, 19
sow, 33, 66–67, 69
spiritual beggar, 66
stewardship, 70
strength, 11
supernatural, 2, 56

T

testimonies, 63
theology, 68
transfer, 28–37
truth, 10, 92

U

Unbelief, 63

V

voice, 19
vows, 11

W

water, 86
wealth, 12, 61, 70–74, 76–80
wisdom, 30, 76
worry, 18, 102
wounds, 20, 83–84

www.ingramcontent.com/pod-product-compliance
Lightning Source LLC
Chambersburg PA
CBHW052152110526
44591CB00012B/1946